CONTENTS

Words that appear in bold, **like this**, are explained in the glossary on page 30.

CULTURE IN JAPAN

A land apart

Curled like a seahorse off the coasts of Korea and Russia, the islands of Japan are the last Asian **landfall** before the Pacific Ocean. Separated from mainland Asia, the Japanese have always seen themselves as different from other Asian countries and cultures.

Legends say that the sun goddess gave birth to the Japanese people at the dawn of time. Some say their ancestors came 2000 years ago in boats from the Pacific islands, others believe they invaded from China. For two thousand years, these people have made Japan their home, developing their unique way of life. Today, Japan's 126 million citizens are extremely proud of their origins, their talents, their ancient culture and the spectacular success of their country.

What is culture?

Culture is a people's way of living. It is the way in which people identify themselves as a group, separate and different from any other. Culture includes a group's language, social customs and habits, as well as its traditions of art, dance, music, writing and religion.

Japan's language, writing, arts and customs have been strongly influenced by its older neighbour, China, but deep in Japanese culture is the drive to be better, faster and smarter. It is a country of achievers with an **ethos** of hard work and a strong sense of duty. Japanese people are generally more comfortable in groups than alone, yet individual passions and needs are brilliantly expressed in the works of Japan's greatest filmmakers and performers.

Alongside all this is a love of beauty, elegance and grace, and a great pride in being Japanese. This is a recipe for success in times of stability, but Japanese people struggle with uncertainty and do not easily accept failure.

an

Melanie Guile

 www.heinemann.co.uk/library
Visit our website to find out more information about Heinemann Library books.

To order:
☎ Phone 44 (0) 1865 888066
🖹 Send a fax to 44 (0) 1865 314091
💻 Visit the Heinemann Bookshop at www.heinemann.co.uk/library to browse our catalogue and order online.

First published 2003 in Australia by Heinemann Library a division of Harcourt Education Australia, 18–22 Salmon Street, Port Melbourne Victoria 3207 Australia (a division of Reed International Books Australia Pty Ltd, ABN 70 001 002 357).

© Reed International Books Australia Pty Ltd 2002
First published in paperback in 2005
The moral right of the publisher has been asserted.

Series cover and text design by Stella Vassiliou
Paged by Stella Vassiliou
Edited by Carmel Heron
Production by Michelle Sweeney

Pre-press by Digital Imaging Group (DIG), Melbourne, Australia
Printed and bound in China by WKT Company Ltd.

ISBN 1 74070 060 0 (hardback)
07 06 05 04 03 02
10 9 8 7 6 5 4 3 2 1

ISBN 0 431 18125 X (paperback)
09 08 07 06 05
10 9 8 7 6 5 4 3 2 1

British Library Cataloguing in Publication Data
Guile, Melanie.
Culture in Japan.
306'.0952
A full catalogue record for this book is available from the British library.

Acknowledgements
Cover photograph of a *kabuki* actor supplied by PhotoDisc.

Other photographs supplied by: Australian Picture Library: pp. 15, 17; Coo-ee Picture Library: p. 29 (top); Japan National Tourist Organisation: pp. 7, 9, 10, 11, 12, 13, 16, 18, 19, 22, 26, 27, 28, 29 (bottom); Kobal Collection/TOHO: p. 21; Michael Sedunary: p. 23; PhotoDisc: pp. 6, 24.

Every attempt has been made to trace and acknowledge copyright. Where an attempt has been unsuccessful, the publisher would be pleased to hear from the copyright owner so any omission or error can be rectified in subsequent printings.

Disclaimer
All the Internet addresses (URLs) given in this book were valid at the time of printing. However, due to the dynamic nature of the Internet, some addresses may have changed, or sites may have ceased to exist since publication. While the author and publisher regret any inconvenience this may cause readers, no responsibility for any such changes can be accepted by either the author or the publisher.

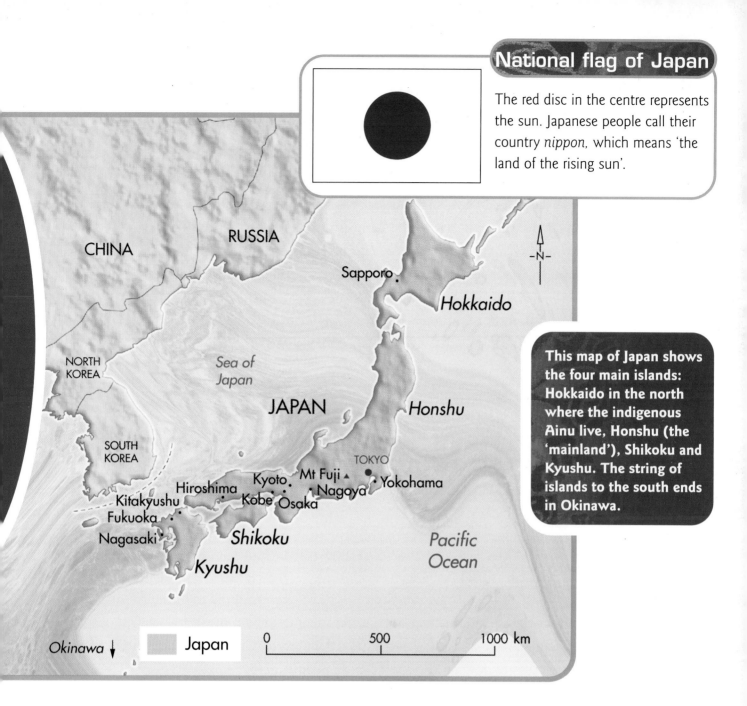

The red disc in the centre represents the sun. Japanese people call their country *nippon*, which means 'the land of the rising sun'.

This map of Japan shows the four main islands: Hokkaido in the north where the indigenous Ainu live, Honshu (the 'mainland'), Shikoku and Kyushu. The string of islands to the south ends in Okinawa.

CHINA

RUSSIA

Sapporo

Hokkaido

NORTH KOREA

Sea of Japan

JAPAN

Honshu

SOUTH KOREA

TOKYO

Kyoto • Mt Fuji ▲

Hiroshima • • Nagoya • Yokohama

Kitakyushu • Kobe • Osaka

Fukuoka • •

Nagasaki • *Shikoku*

Kyushu

Pacific Ocean

Okinawa ↓ [ ] Japan

0   500   1000 km

Monoculture

To Australians used to a **multicultural** society, Japan's culture is astonishingly pure. In fact only one per cent of the people living in Japan are not Japanese, and laws are framed to make it difficult for foreigners to become Japanese citizens. Although they are famously generous and friendly to foreign guests, many Japanese want their culture to remain pure and untainted by outsiders. Being different is generally not encouraged. Minority groups such as the *burakumin* (traditional **outcasts** or 'untouchables') and the **indigenous** Ainu people still suffer **discrimination**.

Traditional symbols

The full moon over Mt Fuji, white-faced *geisha* girls in flowery *kimono* robes, Zen Buddhist temples where monks meditate – these are the traditional symbols of Japanese culture, but they are only a small part of the story.

Today's Japan is fast-moving and competitive. Getting ahead is important – it means dedicating yourself to the company, the club or the school. There is no time to meditate and little space to be alone. But traditions help to reassure Japanese people that old ways have not died. Crowds still gather under the cherry blossoms every year to celebrate spring. Grieving mothers still give offerings of little red bibs to graveside statues for the souls of their dead babies. The old ways give the Japanese a sense of timelessness in a fast-changing world.

Keep cool

Politeness is much more important than telling the blunt truth in Japan. Directly disagreeing with someone is considered bad manners, and getting agitated or angry is definitely 'uncool'. Japanese people are generally reserved and do not like to express strong emotions.

Geisha girls are traditional symbols of Japanese culture.

Times of change

Since their defeat in World War II (1939–1945), the Japanese have proved they can succeed by technical brilliance and hard work. For decades their country created an economic miracle with full employment, high wages and a slick, fast lifestyle.

However, during the last decade or so, growing problems such as unemployment, homelessness, **terrorism** and pollution have made the Japanese question the costs, which include the endless rat-race of school and working life, and the rigid roles required of men and women. Many aspects of Japanese culture today capture the tension between the drive to live and play hard, and the need for peace and rest.

No breaks, thanks

In the past, workers in Japan did not have many holidays. Until recently, it was also considered 'poor form' to take all of the holidays offered. This is changing and the number of holidays is now similar to that enjoyed by workers in other countries.

PERFORMING ARTS

People often judge performances by the talent and flair of individual directors, actors or dancers. In Japan, performance is not necessarily about **showcasing** individuals. It is about preserving traditions and recapturing the perfection of an ancient art.

Kabuki

Kabuki theatre is the people's choice. It dates back to the early 1600s and involves spectacular stage sets and costumes, music and dancing, and popular stories. There is a catwalk stage called a *hanamichi* (flower path) that runs right through the audience.

Action is dramatic and extravagant, and designed to entertain. Performances last all day, meals are brought in, people come and go and the atmosphere is hectic. *Kabuki* means 'song-dance skill', and players must be able to sing, mime, dance and act. Families of *kabuki* actors go back centuries, and it is common for players to put the number of generations after their name. *Kabuki* is still popular today, and performances are held at the Kabuki Theatre and the National Theatre in Tokyo.

Bugaku

Bugaku is the ancient court dance of Japan and has not changed since about AD 700. Several dancers move together in slow, formal movements and poses, accompanied by the traditional *gagaku* orchestra of flutes, strings and drums. The flowing silk costumes are traditionally either red or green, and the dancers wear stiffened hats and white silk slippers and sometimes masks as well. The aim of the dance is to create a sense of harmony and elegance.

Healing music

The musical accompaniment to *bugaku* is the *gagaku* orchestra. Ancient instruments include the *koto*, a 13-stringed 2-metre-long zither that is plucked; the *biwa*, a short-necked lute; two kinds of flutes; and several drums. The musicians sit on the stage to play and are part of the *bugaku* performance, although the music is also sometimes played on its own. The most famous piece is called *etenraku* ('divine music'). It takes up to seven years to learn *gagaku*, and the music is said to bring spiritual healing. *Gagaku* is still played at the emperor's court, but most Japanese today are more familiar with modern music.

A scene from a *No* play – Japan's oldest musical drama dating back to the 1300s

No theatre

No began around AD 1300 in the Emperor's court. The language used in performances today dates back to that period. A *No* play is not meant to be realistic – it is more like a ritual storytelling with movement and mime. Two or three masked actors, plus a chorus of ten singers and four musicians (flute and drums), perform before a backdrop of a pine tree. One actor watches while the main actor tells of some past event or tragedy.

About 2000 *No* scripts survive, and one of the most famous is *Matsukaze* ('Wind in the Pines') by Kan'ami, written in AD 1360. Like western classical ballet, a *No* performance is an elegant and formal kind of stage art. It is much admired by '**highbrow**' audiences in Kyoto and Tokyo.

Puppet theatre

Puppet shows are not always for children. Japan has its own classical puppet theatre dating back to around 1600. *Bunraku* uses nearly life-sized dolls worked by puppeteers, accompanied by a chanted story and music from a three-stringed lute called a *samisen*. The dolls are life-like in their movements and expressions, and it takes three puppeteers on stage to work each one. The stories are often tragic tales from daily life. One of these is *Keisei Awa no Naruto*, which was written in 1769 and is about a mother and her long-lost daughter. Originally puppeteers passed their skills on to only the eldest son, but now non-puppeteering families and women are welcome in *bunraku*.

A *Bunraku* puppet play. The name *bunraku* comes from the Osaka puppeteer Uemura Bunrakuken, who revived the art in the 1800s.

Indigenous music

The Ainu are Japan's indigenous people of Hokkaido, and their music is distinctive. It uses straw whistles, skin drums and flutes. The oldest Ainu music is a type of song called *yukar*, which tells epic stories of gods and ancient heroes.

J-Pop and western-style music

Pop music is huge in Japan, second only to the United States of America in CD sales. As in other countries, image is often more important than talent. Japanese pop (called J-Pop) style is predictable, with cute girl singers and rock bands (with names like Hikky and Shonen Knife) as well as solo artists who have star status in Japan. In the last few years, a reggae–islander sound has appeared on Okinawa, one of Japan's southernmost islands, with groups like Nenes and Champloose.

Western–style music in Japan is not all rock and pop. Classical music is popular, and the Japan Broadcasting Corporation (NHK) sponsors the famous NHK Symphony Orchestra. Popular songs called *kayookyoku* sprang up in the early 1900s. One type of these, called *enka,* were sad-sounding tunes sung with a sob in the voice. Other types of *kayookyoku* were cheerful, happy tunes. Misora Hibari was a famous performer who had hit records from the 1940s to the 1980s. Modern music composer Sakamoto Ryuichi won an **Academy Award** for Best Soundtrack for the film *The Last Emperor* in 1988.

Karaoke

Businessmen, called salarymen, in Tokyo began the craze for **amateur** singing to backing tapes. It was their way of letting off tension from the long office week. Today, *karaoke* is popular and thousands of bars, booths and 'boxes' (specially designed rooms) are swamped by teens and twenty-somethings out to party.

TRADITIONS
and customs

 ## New Year

Long hours of school and work are broken up in Japan with dozens of national and regional festivals. The biggest celebration is *shoogatsu,* or New Year, from 1 to 3 January. The gods are thanked and welcomed into homes with pine and bamboo decorations on either side of the front door. Greeting cards are sent to family and friends – over four billion each New Year! Children are given gifts of money, and families make their first visit of the year to the **Shinto** shrine or temple to pray for health and safety.

 ## Children

Grandparents often live with the family and mind the children while parents work. Very young children are free to play, but once they reach school age, life becomes more competitive, and hard work and discipline are expected. Many children have to sit an exam just to get into kindergarten! 'Cram schools' (*juku*) are essential to get into the best high schools and universities, and the pressure at examination time is brutal.

Cloth carp-fish kites decorate houses on Children's Day

Children's festivals

Several yearly festivals are just for children. *Kodomo-no-hi* on 5 May is Children's Day. Originally just for boys, now all children decorate their houses with cloth carp-fish kites on poles and eat rice dumplings wrapped in bamboo leaves. The fifth day of the fifth month was traditionally unlucky, so *Kodomo-no-hi* helped to banish evil spirits and promote good health for children.

Shichi-Go-San (Seven-Five-Three Festival) is for girls of three and seven and boys of three and five. On 15 November, the children dress in *kimono* and go to the shrine or temple to offer prayers of thanks for having reached that stage of growth. Parents buy them lollies called *chitose-ame* ('thousand years candy') for long life.

On March 3 *Hina-matsuri*, the Doll Festival, is for the health and happiness of little girls. Families display traditionally dressed dolls and decorate the house with peach blossoms, and the girls wear their best *kimono*.

Thousands flock to celebrate spring *hanami* (cherry-tree viewing festival)

Marriage

Japanese couples spend a small fortune on their wedding ceremony and reception. With many families, a family ceremonies is held first at a Shinto shrine (nowadays often a room at the reception centre). The bride wears a white silk *kimono* and the groom a black one. The priest gives offerings to the Shinto spirits, and the couple drink *sake* (rice wine) while the groom (but not the bride) speaks his vows.

The reception afterwards might have 200 guests, including the couple's teachers, bosses and other important figures. Speeches, songs and a meal are enjoyed, and the bride appears in several outfits, often including a western-style wedding dress. Many couples choose to wed overseas because, even including the travel costs, it is cheaper than celebrating at home. Australia and Hawaii are popular choices for Japanese newlyweds.

Indigenous Ainu couples have simpler traditions. When proposing marriage, the man comes to the hut of the girl with a bowl of cooked rice. He eats half and offers the rest to his sweetheart. If she eats it, she accepts his proposal of marriage. If she puts it to one side, she rejects him.

Cherry tree viewing

Thousands of people turn out every weekend in early April to celebrate spring *hanami* (cherry tree viewing festival). This custom of picnicking under the blossom dates back to the 1600s, when poor people gathered for fun and good food outdoors. Today, during *hanami*, television news includes a cherry tree blossom report on the best viewing locations.

AINU CULTURE

The Ainu are the indigenous people of Japan who live on the northern island of Hokkaido. Like Australian Aboriginal people, the Ainu suffer discrimination in their own country. Now they are fighting to preserve their traditional language, culture and way of life.

The people

Traditionally, the Ainu were hunters and gatherers. Many Ainu now farm, fish or work in the tourist trade near Hokkaido's capital city, Sapporo. Around 25 000 people identify themselves as Ainu, but years of discrimination against them mean that many choose to pass as Japanese. Village and family life is important to the Ainu, and they have strong spiritual ties with the land, animals and the natural world.

Owl of ill omen

Beware the horned owl! This night-flying hunter is a bird-demon to the Ainu, and if one flies above you, bad luck is coming. One remedy is to spit as far and fast as possible – this will expel the evil out of your mouth. To see an owl fly across the moon means big trouble. The only way to avoid it is to change your name so that the demon will not know you when he comes.

As in many indigenous communities, Ainu standards of living, health and education are generally poorer than those of the majority of Japanese. Organisations such as the Ainu International Network are trying to improve standards. In 1997, the Japanese Parliament finally recognised the cultural rights of the Ainu by passing the *Act for Encouragement of Ainu Culture and **Diffusion** and **Enlightenment** of Knowledge of Ainu Traditions*. Unfortunately, the Act does not recognise **land rights**.

Dances

To the Ainu, dance is a way of thanking the gods. The *upopo* is an introduction to a celebration in which women sit in a circle and sing to the beat of drums. *Rimse*, which means 'banging sound', is a dance and song to scare away evil spirits after a disaster. Villagers wave swords and stamp their feet as they move among the houses. One of the few dances for men is the *emush rimse* – a kind of sword duel where two men slash at each other with great energy and skill to a chorus of shouts and encouragement from the audience.

Clothing

Finely decorated costumes are worn for dances and special ceremonies. Striking geometric patterns of red, white, black and blue are sewn onto cloth and made into coats and trousers. Traditional clothes were made of bird or fish skins, and bark fabric called *attush* made from elm trees is still worn. Modern Ainu women wear a traditional all-in-one body suit as underwear, which is put on over the head. Embroidered headbands are worn like hats, and metal hoop and ball earrings are threaded through pierced ears. Chunky glass bead necklaces with metal medallions, called *tamasai*, are for special occasions.

An indigenous Ainu man. The Ainu are culturally distinct from the Japanese. 'Ainu' means 'human' in the Ainu language.

FASHION

A sense of style

The Japanese have always been fashion-conscious. Around AD 800, when Europeans wore rough and greasy home-spun clothes, wealthy Japanese bathed daily and dressed themselves in richly patterned robes (*kimono*). Their sense of neatness and style remains today. Japanese fashion designers, such as Yohji Yamamoto with his sophisticated Y's label, have gained international recognition. Incomes are high in Japan, and much money is spent on looking good.

Tradition with a twist

The elaborate and beautiful *kimono*, Japan's national dress, is still worn at weddings, New Year and coming-of-age ceremonies. The *kimono* has 12 parts, including special underwear, layers of silk robes and the *obi*, a 3-metre-long stiff sash. Thongs decorated with silk, called *zoori*, and toed socks, called *tabi*, are worn, and strict rules dictate how a woman sits, bows and walks. A kimono can take up to two hours to put on and can cost as much as a small car!

Not surprisingly, many modern women and girls are shunning traditional dress, but designers are fighting back. New *kimono* designs include features such as velcro, zips and wash-and-wear fabrics. Lightweight summer *kimono* called *yukata* are the basis of a fashion revival. New interpretations include the mini-*yukata*, worn with platform wooden thongs, and a mosquito-proof *yukata*, treated with the chemical tropolone to kill summer pests!

The *kimono* is Japan's national dress and is still worn for important occasions.

Street wear

Every weekend in Tokyo's Shibuya neighbourhood, thousands of teens in wild gear gather to hang out, be seen and be photographed. These are the *ganguro* girls and their boyfriends. Their fantastic outfits began as a protest against old-fashioned Japanese views of women as quiet and modest. Micro-mini skirts, huge platform shoes, brilliant colours, tanned skin with white eyeliner, and bleached or pigtailed hair make up the look. Department stores now stock this **street wear** under labels such as Bathing Ape and Hysteric Glamour. Although the *ganguro* girls look startlingly different, in fact they follow strict dress codes dictated by their own 'style tribes'.

Warm inner glow

Short sleeves are 'in', but how to stay both warm and fashionable in Japan's sub-zero winters? Japanese scientists have come up with 'high-tech' underwear. New fabrics include ceramic particles that give off **infrared** radiation to keep the wearer warm.

Ganguro girls in Tokyo. In 1999, a 23-year-old girl died of a fractured skull when she fell off her platform shoes, and the Japanese Government issued an official warning against them.

FOOD

Like many aspects of Japanese culture, pleasing harmony, or *wa,* is the key to eating in Japan. Traditionally, food must have three aspects: it should look beautiful, be finely presented, and of course it should taste good. Ingredients are fresh, lightly cooked or raw, and barely spiced so that the pure taste of the food comes through. Traditional foods are rice, seafood, vegetables, seaweed and soya beans, but today every kind of **exotic** food is available in Japan.

Rice

In the Japanese language, the word for 'meal' – *gohan* – means 'rice' (just as we might say 'daily bread'). Once rice was a form of currency, and **samurai** warriors were paid in rice. Bowls of rice are offered to the dead at Shinto religious festivals, and *sake* is drunk during rituals and to greet important guests. Some scholars believe that the cooperation between farmers that was necessary to grow rice was the origin of the strong need to belong to a group that characterises Japanese culture. However, statistics show that Japanese people are eating less rice today. Japan now imports billions of dollars of raw food every year, although it is a matter of great pride to them that they still grow enough rice to feed themselves.

Fast food

Pizza and sandwiches are popular choices for a quick lunch, or you can pop out for a *Mosburger*, a popular hamburger, at one of the thousands of hamburger and other food outlets in Japan's crammed and humming cities. Beautifully packed lunch boxes called *bento* offer students and workers a ready-made takeaway meal. Cans of hot coffee, milky, strong and very sweet, can be bought at vending machines. Every train station has fast food outlets to cater for **commuters**. Businessmen might snatch a quick meal of noodles late at night on their way home from the office.

A sushi platter. Visual appeal is extremely important in Japanese culture.

 # Eating out

Restaurants tend to specialise in one kind of food. Noodle bars serve *soba*, which are thin, brown buckwheat noodles served in a fish broth. You can have them plain with dipping sauce, or in many other ways. A combination with tofu, spring onions or a raw egg is called *tsukimi soba* (which means moon-gazing!). *Udon* is similar to *soba* but these wheat noodles are thick and white. The famous *sushi* bars sell beautifully prepared rice and fish morsels wrapped in seaweed. *Sashimi* is a popular meal consisting of strips of raw fish served with soy sauce and *wasabi* (horseradish).

Forbidden food

Eating red meat was forbidden in Japan until 1867, when Emperor Meiji opened up the country to foreign influences. Today, most older Japanese still prefer white meat or seafood, although Kobe beef is an expensive delicacy often used in the famous dish *sukiyaki*. Younger Japanese enjoy burgers made from Australian and US beef.

School and work are demanding in Japan, so videos and television are generally light escapes from the grind of daily life. Nonetheless, many Japanese film directors are highly regarded by serious critics.

Early films

Japanese filmmakers produced their first film in 1898. Popular silent movie themes were the deeds of *samurai* warriors and heroes. Instead of subtitles, actors were hired to do a spoken commentary on the silent action. The Japanese miliary used sound films for **propaganda**, but after World War II films began to attract attention as an art form.

Golden age of film

Three brilliant film directors established the golden age of Japanese film in the 1950s. Kenji Mizoguchi (1898–1956) trained as an artist, which shows in his beautiful camera work. His intense film *The Life of Oharu* dramatises a woman's downfall, and won international praise. The films of Yasujiro Ozu (1903–1963) focus on ordinary Japanese working people and the **suppression** of true feelings. His famous film *Tokyo Story* (1953) is often rated among the ten best films ever made.

Akira Kurosawa's (1910–1998) career spanned almost 50 years. Known for their spectacular camera work, funny and moving plots and great characters, Kurosawa's films have been copied around the world. *Rashomon* (1950), which is about an attack on a woman told from four different viewpoints, won first prize at the Venice Film Festival. His 1954 film *Shichinin-no-Samurai* (*The Seven Samurai*) is about a band of warriors who save a town from bandits, and is one of the most admired works in film history. The successful Hollywood film *The Magnificent Seven* is a remake of it.

Reality TV

Reality TV show 'Sata Suma' sends a 'maid' to selected viewers' homes to surprise busy families and do the morning's housework. The maid's cheery greeting *'oh-ha!'* is short for *ohayo gozaimasu* (good morning), and it has become the latest way to greet friends at school. But the maid is actually a man – he is 23-year-old pop star Shingo Katori of the pop group SMAP. So popular is the show that *oh-ha* was awarded a government prize for 'trendy word of 2000', and the Minister of Education invited Shingo to promote the government's 'talk with our children' campaign!

The new generation

Television and video devastated filmmaking in Japan. From a peak audience of 1.1 billion in 1958, films now attract around 120 million viewers a year. But a new wave of film directors is fighting back. Takeshi Kitano (known as 'Beat' Takeshi) is the biggest media personality in Japan. He has eight television programs a week, and regular radio and newspaper spots. He began his career as a stand-up comedian in the 1970s, but now writes, directs and acts in his own films. *Sonatine* (1993) won praise at the Cannes Film Festival, but his most famous film is *Hana Bi (Fireworks)* (1997), which is a violent film about a corrupt police officer and gangsters and what happens after a police shoot-out.

Itami Juzo (1933–1997) began his career as an actor and then turned to directing. His comedies like *Marusa no Onna* (*A Taxing Woman*) show the social and political quirks of modern Japan.

Animated praise

Animated films (*anime*) make up one-third of all box office takings in Japan. *My Neighbour Totoro* (1988), by Hayao Miyazaki, is a well-animated, heart-warming story about two little girls who discover the magical spirits of a forest. Critics claimed it took animated films to a new level of excellence.

BOOKS, *magazines and comics*

Japan has the highest literacy rate in the world – almost 100 per cent of people can read and write. This skill does not go to waste as the Japanese are avid readers of books, papers, magazines and *manga* (comics), and also have a long tradition of fine literature.

Classic literature

The Tale of the Genji by Lady Murasaki Shibiku was written around AD 1000. It is a story of life, love and secret plotting at the Emperor's court and is regarded as Japan's greatest classic. A much loved travel book by the poet Matsuo Basho is *The Narrow Road to the Deep North*. Modern fans of his book still climb the three mountain peaks described in his journey. Japan's greatest modern writer is Natsume Soseki (1867–1916). He was a lecturer in English at Tokyo University in the early 1900s, but gave up his job to write. One of his more famous novels is *Kokoro* (meaning 'feelings' or 'the heart'). Written in 1914, it is a sad story about loneliness and betrayal. Kawabata Yasunari (1899–1972), who wrote the famous story, *Snow Country*, won the Nobel Prize for literature in 1948.

Haiku

Japanese culture values simplicity and subtlety, and the *haiku* form of poetry expresses both. In just 17 **syllables,** the writer must express deep emotions, often about the beauty of nature. The moon, falling cherry blossoms and snowy Mt Fuji are popular subjects.

One of Japan's greatest modern writers, Natsume Soseki, features on the 1000 **yen** banknote.

Bookshops in Japan stock thousands of types of *manga*. One-quarter of all books published in Japan are comics.

Mad about *manga*

Manga (meaning 'playful pictures') is the Japanese word for 'comics'. Japanese people read more *manga* than any other country in the world. In Australia comics are for children, but in Japan there are special comics for teenagers (*shonenshi*), for young adults (*yangushi*) and even for business people. *Manga* are like films or novels, with complex story-lines and characters. Japanese *manga* artists are famous for their skill and inventiveness, and they are treated like pop stars. Over six million *manga* are read every week. The most popular is *Shonen Jump*.

'Father' of Japanese manga

The first comics appeared in Japan around AD 700, but they only took off after World War II in 1945. The man responsible for their popularity is Japan's greatest *manga* artist Tezuka Osamu (1926–1989). He was inspired by Walt Disney and saw the animated film *Bambi* 80 times! Tezuka created the world-famous characters of Astro Boy (*Tetsuwan Atomu*) in 1963 and Kimba the White Lion in 1965. He drew 150 000 comic strips in his lifetime and started the modern craze for comics and animated films (*anime*) in Japan. A museum in Osaka is dedicated to Tezuka.

Millions of newspapers

More than 50 million newpapers are sold daily in Japan. The daily *Yomiuri Shimbun* has the largest circulation of any daily paper in the world with over ten million readers.

KIDS' CULTURE

Fads

Fads come and go in Japan, especially among teenagers and schoolchildren. While older people value Japan's ancient traditions, young people go mad for anything new and different. One in three Japanese owns a mobile phone, and young people treat them as fashion accessories. **Gimmicks** include plug-in receivers shaped like shoes, and ballpoint pens or teddy bears that flash or move when a call is received.

A new craze called '365 Days Birthday Teddy' has captured girls' imaginations. Inside every chocolate bar is a small, brightly patterned bear – a different one for every day of the year. Naturally, girls want to get the bear with their own birth date, but there is no way of telling what date is there until you open the box. The demand for the chocolate treats is so great that manufacturers cannot keep up.

Japanese school children love anything new and different. Recent fads include electronic games and toys, as well as an ancient Chinese boardgame

Hi-tech toys

Japan leads the world in high-tech goods so it is no surprise that some of the most popular electronic games were invented by the Japanese. Nintendo Co. Ltd., of Kyoto, launched its first home video game system in 1985. It became an instant success. Nearly 20 years later, the games are more powerful and complex, but the action adventure formula is the same.

The creation of the Pokemon® characters extended the fame of Nintendo. More than 250 cute, animal-like creatures feature in video games, on swap cards and cartoons. Popular characters such as Pikachu are collected by kids all over Japan and around the world.

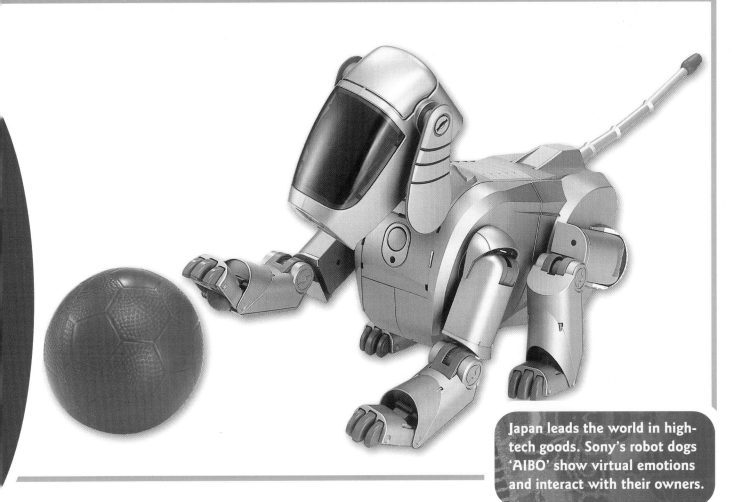

Japan leads the world in high-tech goods. Sony's robot dogs 'AIBO' show virtual emotions and interact with their owners.

The craze for *tamagotchi* began in Japan in 1996 when the toymaker Bandai Co., created the idea of 'virtual toys'. These palm-sized, egg-shaped electronic gadgets were programmed to behave like living pets, demanding food, sleep or cuddles. Girls in particular were so distracted by their *tamagotchi* that they could not concentrate on their studies, and schools banned them. Recent updates on this theme are robots (human and animal) that show **virtual** emotions and **interact** realistically with their owners.

Go

Go is an ancient Chinese boardgame for two using black and white stones on a wooden board. Usually played by older people, *go* has taken off among schoolchildren. The reason is a *manga* comic strip called *Shukan Shonen Janpu* (*Weekly Jump*). In the comic called *Hikaru no go*, a boy named Hikaru learns to play the game from a phantom *go* master. In 2000, the Japan Go Association had 16 000 school children turn up to its annual *go* competition and had to turn hundreds away.

Hard yards

Japanese schoolchildren are expected to clean their yards, classrooms, halls and toilets every day. Teachers expect obedience and no talking in class. After-school clubs are popular for sporting and artistic activities, but some make for a 12-hour school day.

ARTS AND CRAFTS

The Japanese artistic sense is understated, minimal and exquisite. Some say this reflects the influence on Japanese arts and crafts of Zen Buddhism, a religion that values simplicity, inner calm and self-denial. Certainly refined good taste is admired above rich, showy extravagance. This can be seen in everyday things like the beautifully carved radish flowers at a *sushi* bar or the bare elegance of a temple rock garden in Kyoto.

Master potters are honoured in Japan as 'living national treasures'.

Painting

Painting has always been popular in Japan. Clear open spaces, fine detail and simple subjects like flowers, birds and landscapes are typical of the Japanese style of painting. Until the 20th century the Japanese wrote with a brush, so ink painting came naturally. Early pictures show a strong Chinese influence, but around AD 1600 a classic style emerged with gold-leaf backgrounds and rich colours painted on folding screens. Hangings often showed people and scenes from court life.

Wood-block prints

Only noblemen could afford original artworks, but in around 1600, wood-block printing meant pictures could be printed cheaply and *ukiyo-e* (woodcut prints) became popular. Each image was first drawn on tracing paper by the artist. The engraver then carved it in raised relief on a block of wood. Finally, the printer ran the paper over the inked block to produce the picture. Subjects were entertainers and pleasure-seekers in the entertainment area of old Edo (today's Tokyo). Many wood-block prints were pictures of *kabuki* actors, an early kind of pop poster. *Ukiyo-e* means 'floating world', named after the frivolous subjects represented. These prints were not treated as artworks at the time; they were enjoyed, then thrown away or used as wrapping paper. Today *ukiyo-e* fetch huge prices at art auctions.

China and pottery

Japanese pottery is world famous, and the designs, shapes and finishes are beautiful. The word for pottery is *setomono* after the town Seto, where the first **kiln** opened in AD 1242. Kyoto is the centre for the famous *raku-yaki* designs. *Raku* means 'enjoy', and this character (word) appears as decoration on the bowls for the tea ceremony. Finer, lighter porcelain came to Japan from Korea in 1598. It was exported to Europe for more than 100 years before people in the **West** discovered how to make it. Distinctive finishes are white crackle glazes and a rich red and black lacquer effect. Master potters today are honoured in Japan as 'living national treasures'.

An artist adds a pattern to a bowl

Home decorating

Underground at Shinjuku station in Tokyo, office workers rush past makeshift cardboard shacks where homeless men shelter. Unemployment was unknown in Japan until the 1990s, when joblessness left former salarymen with nowhere else to live. There is no pension in Japan, and without family support, people easily drop out. Resisting police attempts to remove them in 1995, the men painted vivid murals on their cardboard house walls. One master artist, Yamamura-san, supervises and coordinates dozens of paintings on the cardboard-box homes. Now the public and critics have taken notice and are opposing further attempts to remove the homeless artists.

The art of living things

In Japan, love of nature is important. Because most people could never afford a private garden, many artistic forms aim to bring the spirit and peace of nature indoors.

The ancient art of *bonsai* involves growing miniature trees. Saplings are shaped with copper wire and root-pruned to look like full-grown, tiny trees. They are planted in shallow pots to show off their roots and branches. Any fruit or flowers appear at normal size. *Bonsai* trees can last for hundreds of years.

Ikebana developed in the 1400s as part of the tea ceremony when *samurai* warriors learned patience, tolerance and love of nature through arranging flowers. The aim is to produce a pleasing harmony between the flowers, the container and the setting. Withered branches, seed pods and fruit are used as well as blooms. Strict rules apply to the shape and style of each arrangement, and different schools of *ikebana* flourish in Japan and throughout the world.

The art of *ikebana* uses plant material to bring the form and beauty of nature indoors.

The Japanese have been gardening for centuries. In the Zen Buddhist religion, gardens are valued for meditation and inner peace. There are three main Japanese garden types: *tsukiyama*, which is a hill garden with water ponds and bridges; *chaniwa*, which is a garden that surrounds a traditional tea house; and *kare-sansui*, which means 'dry river-bed' and is a remarkable stone and raked sand garden that has no plants at all. The most famous *kare-sansui* is the walled garden of the Ryoan-ji Temple in Kyoto. Set out in 1499, its 15 large rocks are placed so that whichever way you view them, one of the rocks is always hidden.

Body art

In the west, tattoos are not regarded as art. However, in Japan, the ancient Japanese form of body art (*irezumi*) takes the whole body as a canvas for the *horishi* (tattoo master). Designs are large and flowing with subtle colouring and great detail. Popular themes include tigers, flowers, folk heroes, dragons for happiness, and the *koi* carp fish, the traditional symbol of courage and success. The tattoos are hand-applied using vegetable dyes and **soot** and take from one to ten years to complete!

In the 1600s, criminals in Japan were tattooed as a punishment and the art is still popular among the Japanese *yakuza* (organised criminals). Modern western-style tattoos are machine applied and use motifs such as Disney characters. Because they use only one point of the body, they are called *wan-pointo* and are looked down upon by the tattoo masters.

Traditional Japanese tattoos called *irezumi* cover the body from neck to knees and take up to ten years to complete.

The garden of the Ryoan-ji Temple in Kyoto. Children on school trips visit and try to work out a way to see all of the 15 rocks.

'Prince of the knitting world'

Hand knitting has become popular thanks to knitwear designer and instructor Mitsuharu Hirose. This celebrity hand knits and models his own garments, runs his own TV show and fashion magazines, and gets floods of fan letters. Answering critics of male knitters as 'sissies', Mitsuharu Hirose asserts, '...being different is alright'.

GLOSSARY

Academy Award   award given in the USA for excellence in films

amateur   done for the love of it and not for money; not professional

animated   cartoons

commuters   people who travel daily to and from work

diffusion   spreading around

discrimination   when people are treated unfairly on the basis of their race, gender or religion, or for some other reason

enlightenment   complete understanding

ethos   a belief or attitude characteristic of a particular group of people, community or system

exotic   strange or bizarre; introduced from abroad

fad   a fashion or craze that only lasts for a short time

geisha   a Japanese girl who entertains with singing, dancing and conversation

gimmick   a clever trick or fad designed to grab people's attention

highbrow   cultured, intellectual

indigenous   original or native to a particular country or area

infrared   invisible rays beyond the end of the light spectrum

interact   actively participate

kiln   an oven used for making pottery

landfall   first land reached after a long sea journey; last land left before a long sea journey

land rights   the right to occupy and use your own land

multicultural   to be made up of several different races and cultures

outcasts   people of no caste or class; rejected by society

propaganda   information (often biased) that is used to convince people of a certain opinion or point of view

samurai   traditional soldiers or warriors in Japan

Shinto   a religion of Japan based on nature and ancestor worship

showcasing   promoting; showing something or someone off

soot   black ashes from a fire

street wear   fashionable clothes for wearing in the street

suppression   stopping something from happening or being seen, heard or known

syllables   a word or the part of a word that has one separate sound when you say it

terrorism   the use of violent acts to put pressure on the government of a nation or state to do what you want

virtual   like the real thing; a term used for life-like experiences created by computers

West   Europe, as opposed to the East or Asia

yen   the Japanese unit of currency

Zen Buddhism   school of Buddhist religion that is popular in Japan; Zen Buddhism teaches followers to meditate in order to understand the truth about the way things are

FURTHER *information*

Books

McCullogh, J. *A World of Recipes* series – *Japan*. Heinemann Library, Oxford, 2001.

Poisson, B. *First Peoples* series – *Ainu of Japan*. Times Editions, Singapore, 2002.

Whyte, H. *Countries of the World* series – *Japan*. Times Editions, Singapore, 1998.

Whyte, H. and N. Frank. *Welcome to my Country* series – *Japan*. Times Editions, Singapore, 1999.

Websites

Modern Japanese culture: jin.jcic.or.jp/today/culture.html

Kids Web Japan: www.jinjapan.org/kidsweb

INDEX